MURDER
Ballad

Murder *Ballad*

JANE SPRINGER

ALICE JAMES BOOKS | FARMINGTON, MAINE

10 9 8 7 6 5 4 3 2 1

Alice James Books are published by Alice James Poetry Cooperative, Inc.,
an affiliate of the University of Maine at Farmington.

ALICE JAMES BOOKS
238 MAIN STREET
FARMINGTON, ME 04938
www.alicejamesbooks.org

Library of Congress Cataloging-in-Publication Data
Springer, Jane.
 Murder ballad / by Jane Springer.
    p. cm.
 ISBN 978-1-882295-93-7 (pbk.)
 I. Title.
 PR9199.4.S7954M87 2012
 811'.6--DC23

                      2011049177

Alice James Books gratefully acknowledges support from individual donors,
private foundations, the University of Maine at Farmington, and the
National Endowment for the Arts.

ART WORKS.
arts.gov

COVER ART: "Nachtszene Gross" Michael Hutter

Contents

Acknowledgments

Grateful acknowledgment is due to the editors of the following literary magazines and online publications where these poems (or altered versions of them) appeared or are forthcoming:

The Cincinnati Review: "Pretty Polly" (published as "Murder Ballad") and "Whiskey Pastoral"

Cavalier Magazine: "Face That Could Pull a Stump"

Connotation Press: An Online Artifact: "Calvary Letter," "Deepfreeze at the House of Boo," "Don't Let Your Mouth Write a Check Your Butt Can't Cash" and "Letter to the Dark"

Fogged Clarity: "Hindsight's Ballad"

Fugue: "The Last Resort"

The Gettysburg Review: "Ether" and "You Want Fair? The Fair Comes in the Fall"

Indiana Review: "Stars, As the Bride Who Could Not Tie the Knot Sees Them" (published as "Stars, As the Bride Who Might Have Been Sees Them") (runner up for the Jeffery E. Smith Prize)

Margie: "Tying the Knot"

New Letters: "Crazing," "Ingénue" (published as "Playing Spin the Bottle in the New Life Church") and "Salt Hill"

Oxford American "The Best of the South" Issue: "What We Call This Frog Hunting"

Pleiades: "Small Cosmos"

Plume: "Leave It Lay Where Jesus Flung It"

Poetry Daily: "Pretty as You Please" (reprint)

Pushcart Prize Anthology XXXVI: "Pretty Polly" (published as "Murder Ballad") (reprint)

Smartish Pace: "You Can't Tell Nobody Nothing Who Ain't Ever Been Nowhere"

The Southern Review: "Snow Angel," "I'll Wear the Hound out of That," "A Coon's Age," "Looks Like the Hound Who Caught the Car," "Nocturne: So Mixed Up She Don't Know Day from Dark" and "Pretty as You Please"

Special thanks also, to the NEA and Whiting Foundations for awarding me fellowships in 2009 and 2010, respectively. I could not have completed this book without their generous support. If I knew the names of the nominators and judges I would have each here.

I'm also indebted to the Alice James Books editorial board for choosing this book for the Beatrice Hawley Award.

To Hamilton College and especially Patrick Reynolds and Margaret Gentry who approved research funds for a cabin where I wrote the backbone of the book, thank you.

Many colleagues, poets and friends deserve credit for helping me shape this book: Naomi Guttman, Margie Thickstun, George Bhalke and James Bradley Wells (from my Hamilton writing group); Carey Salerno, Monica A. Hand, Meg Willing and Frank Giampietro (from Alice James Books); April Ossmann (freelance editor); and Mike Carson and Connie Myers (friends and mentors from University of Evansville). Two poets, in particular, worked closely with me on building the form and content of this manuscript: Dave Smith: Thank you, David, for the tough love and advice that helped these poems (hopefully) become stronger. James Kimbrell: I appreciate, so much, your spending months (years) helping to shape this and all my manuscripts, as is your generous nature to do so.

Thanks to my family: John, Morrison and all. Dad, thank you for allowing me to use (and alter!) your wonderful stories. Without them the book would lack a certain depth of character, which you have in abundance.

Tenderly, for Dad.

I

You've got to have something to eat and a little love in your life
before you can hold still for any damn body's sermon
on how to behave.

—BILLIE HOLIDAY

Face That Could Pull a Stump

For besides beaver teeth,
       my love had more pocks on
              his face than a watermelon

has seeds. New rain falling
       on the tub of leaf covered
              corn by our feet—loam

squished up between our
       toes—so I think our tracks
              became the fossilized map

of where we walked through
       broom sage thicket & pecan
              grove to get to where we

stood that night—aiming a
       flashlight's beam up sky
              bayous of splayed tree limbs—

spider eyes glinting like hot
       star-planets & silvery tails
              of moss comets, caught

midfire in the branches. He
        angled his father's twenty-
                two toward a coon he'd

treed in the crook of the
        trunk & we could hear an
                owl *woo* the animal through

a universe so foreign & deep
        we neither fathomed the
                span of its wings, nor what

strange custom carried its
        voice to the woods where the
                boy had found—bright hills—

my hips & strung me with
        a necklace of hickeys so I
                was bound to the moment

by its unspent bullets, webbed
        branches teeming with eyes,
                the ugly boy whose face I loved

& the wooing owl who flew
        off with the coon in her talons
                before we could shoot her down.

What We Call This Frog Hunting

This is the last 2 A.M. song fit for poling a johnboat through the swamp
so we may glide, quiet enough, to catch frogs with our hands.

It's the year Robertlee can't afford a suit to take me to prom.

Our flashlights tell the difference between alligators & sunken logs
adrift in the dark.

This year Emmyjean's daddy shows us how he guts a deer.

As for the girls, we'd rather be kissing. We've practiced our kissing
on each other—shy as spotted fawns.

We know the boys sometimes meet for a circlejerk in an empty barn.

This is the canvas bag we keep frogs in, once they are caught. It
will hold thirteen by dawn.

It's the year we learn to sew a pleat & stew a coon in Home Ec.

T.J. Corbett has such long arms—the boat don't tip when he leans out
over the rim.

This year, we can't all read well enough to fill in class ring forms.

We've never been so aware of skin—the full bag is an organ beating
on the floor of the boat.

                  We barely contain our joy.

This is the year the principal measures the acre between our knees
& the hems of our skirts.

We dock the boat & break the backs of frogs against a stone.

We know they are dead when their tongues unfurl. This is the last
newborn light licked between cypress trunks.

Lunch ladies from here serve fried okra & jambalaya.

The round spot behind each animal eye is an ear—here we circle
the head's globe with a single knifeslice.

Though all year we've swerved to miss guineas by the schoolyard.

We push our thumbs under the edge of skin at the throat to loosen
slick bodies from the green.

This is the year: the dark, the boat, the sunken suits & watery forms,

the catch & kiss, damp canvas, split rib, dawn & entrails in the grass—
we cut the feet last—in the pleated heat—

       then wipe our blades across our thighs & call this happiness.

Looks Like the Hound Who Caught the Car

Is how you pace the hardware store
        asking the man for a sheet of glass
the kind they don't make anymore
        for your back door when you don't
have two nickels to rub together.

Last week you thought she came
        down the road like a Tennessee
Walker, finer than froghair, a tall
        drink of water—so you bought
her a wax job, chrome hubcaps

& bet the prizehog you could get
        in her pants—then dug out a fence
(why the perimeter of your yard
        is a mile long trench) & hauled ass
after her bumper down I-10. Not

like you to turn tail for a whistle or
        holler home. Crazy as a shithouse
rat—by week's end she'd bought
        the dress & borrowed blue to marry
you—who change your mind a day

late & a dollar short. Is why her
        bocce balls landed like three burned
out engines on your kitchen floor,
        while your new live-in stoked lover's
grits & made the appointment to have

you fixed. What you woofed at weren't
        after all, the best tennisball breasts in
the sweethereafter, but headlights. It's
        why your ears resemble windblown
tracks & you hack up asphalt (though

your fur shines with a halogen brilliance).

You Want Fair? The Fair Comes in the Fall

The brick tied to the freshman's scrotum for initiation was knotted
to slip off, but he didn't know this—blindfolded & naked

on the table he must have remembered the castration

of goats done before fairs so bucks will not commit crude acts such
as pissing in their own beards to attract she-goats. How

we learned decorum those years had so much to do

with Oscar Milby's ballsack—he did not go back to Bethel's college
of books after that & boys gossiped in hallways: *Sissy*—

the livestock synonym for the human animal

who bites & kicks his way out of a herd of blue-ribboned show goats
to wander into the alien forest.

To the boys who held the brick-to-scare-the-Jesus

out of Milby, I suppose, *Fair's in the fall* meant they would continue
their studies in Greek & Latin in the seminary of autumn

in an effort to tap the foreign root of justice & compassion.

Such rites of passage back then were the fashion—much as every boy
wore the same military flattop & block letterman's jacket,

formica tables styled every mother's kitchen.

& being born to the farm, Oscar Milby would have known that once
you cinch the tourniquet around a buck's sack it takes

two weeks for the gonads to lose blood, gangrene, hit dirt—

so that even as the shock wore off from his passed initiation—the knot
slipped, the brick
dropped—

his hands felt—in his own soft pouches—an animal warmth

that was, for him, worth leaving school to preserve. Whether or not Milby's
fleeing led him to more fertile ground I cannot say—his

name's not penned with ours in the county records. As if he

was by our shame—erased. I want to believe this: Each yellow leaf
that fell that year was his forgiveness—his fled footprint—

the autumn light, shifting.

You Can't Tell Nobody Nothing Who Ain't Never Been Nowhere

That something to tell lays wait   this side of the gate
that's all chigger,   no shade.

Or is haloed in the tender   mule's hoof,
before concussion.

Like the child pretending
      to brush her new teeth
           or the one who dreams of   joining the army.

& poor John Henry.
If   (only).

When first learning to peel beets,   it feels right to cut—
blade aimed   toward spleen.

But you have to see for   yourself.

In unripe persimmons
      that look sweet or your
           feet arched to dive off   the interstate bridge.

In the gas station passed   between a full tank
& a flare in the bayou.

(Though your

                                    mother warned you.)

Down yonder a stretch,   veer right,
      go a piece & it's down
             aways to the left.   In the wrong exit.

Or the girl's leg, washed   to riverbank reeds—
wherever—   alone—

                                          was she going?

Hindsight's Ballad: I'd Go Back & Fix Me, If I Was My Own Daughter

æ

Now all is one highway. One combine, yellow, so long settled in dirt—crows make
　　　　a disco of it. One logging truck, the Merritt's, one cropduster whose circular sweep
of blue smoke is the summer's news.

Your moving truck cuts through cotton barbed to prick fingers that pluck it & flat pasture
　　　　where cows stand mucked up to their ankles in mudponds—ghostcows drawn with
skeletal ribs & haunches.

Humidity here will swamp the average while wind speed sticks on still, large motorized
　　　　vehicle count: Sixteen. This is no Memphis. Camelback houses, shotgun doubles,
front yard chickens, cockfight

Wednesday, Dixie Dandy Grocery sells catfish bloodbait, bright orange hats, gas, bullets.
　　　　I see you open parsonage cabinets already filled with dry goods from the pounding
thrown for your family's arrival:

Sacks of flour, cream of tartar, grits—four cardboard shakers of Creole hot stuff. You've
　　　　never used newspaper for tablecloth, sucked the head & eaten the tail of crawfish,
known two dollar wine tasted so pink.

～

One body—yours.

Is the hot new jackoff topic in every men's bathroom. Which makes things multiply.
　　　　I see you in black jeans with two holes torn out the knees & a three-stringed
halter that shows what a scant

mile you believe you could walk on your smarts. What you don't know: No one wants you
　　　　drunk to hear you recite the high school mercy speech from *Merchant of Venice* & that
dirt road carved through one

pitchblack mile of swampgrass will not lead you to the Julliard your aunt & mother put
　　　　money in your savings for—but to a shack small as a four-walled dock
& about as stable.

I would tell you not to go in. Or rope you like a calf & lock you in a trunk till dawn
　　　　if that's what it took not to watch you down those crown & cokes—throw your
fivers in the air & laugh—

your paper money falling by the barstool. Your snowy egret breasts. Your limbs akimbo
　　　　across the pool table or in the back parking lot where you will go limp, deaf
& dumb for six men

who will square you up under them casually as if laying down bricks or digging gravedirt.

    After this, you will see their faces at night, you will piss your bed, you will carry a steak knife

        in your purse.

∾

At sixteen, you kneel to touch letters on a plantation stone: *Bill Chase/A Beloved And/ Faithful Slave.* I have some questions for

Mr. Chase: What name did your birth
    mother palm onto your crown & was
        she then sold down the Mississippi? How
           could I love the river if this were so—

           river at sixteen, I think I know? Rich
        black with delta sediment—river who
    could carry a cypress three thousand miles
on its back & still not ache—who floods,

fathoms & contains as weather designs.
    Whose currents copper in the deep
        draught of afternoon sun & who moves
           the temporal shore. Bill Chase, I want to

know if you haunt the places that hurt you—
here in Newellton? Do you retrace fields
for one last look at your sons & daughters—
the boy you were at sixteen? Or do you go,

now, like the river goes—breaking through
levees as you see fit, calling up storms to
frighten Zeus, letting poor fishermen think it's
luck—not you—who wash fish to their feet?

Maybe you are the patron saint of lost girls
caught in the wrong bar with their drawers
pulled to their ankles and you can avenge me.
You, who in life could have been tied to a stump

& hot tar poured on your balls then set aflame
for raising an eyebrow in the wrong direction?
Do you have enough lightning left in you to
brand the cheek of the barman whose face

was one bad freckle? Could you shackle the
one who said *sorry* to his wife's bed frame? How
long would it take to scalp the third one if you
tied his mullet to a tractor & dredged him through

gravel? Could you nail horse shoes to the hands
& feet of the one with the rodeo buckle—
or maim, with a shovel, the one who knuckled me
in place? Maybe you could stick a meat hook

through the solar plexus of man number six
& lift his body to the trees till his blood drains
& he becomes the carrion special stripped by
birds to skeletal remains? Your marker must

get hot as brimstone out here with no shade.
Maybe it is just a stone & you are not a god—
but one dead human. Were you alone like me
in Newellton—wanting a plot of land to own

where no one would correct, with a whip, what
crop you planted in crooked rows? With someone
to trust your secrets to, who would not ask *why*?
But make a balm for you & say: *I'm on your side.*

I will neither call you Bill Chase, nor beloved,
nor slave. Neither will I call you ghost, river, rain—
these are not your name. I cannot fathom
either your source or end any better than I

can keep my own body from falling where
you lay—or keep my hands from touching
this stone. My shadow separates from me as if
she never belonged to me. Maybe our pluvial

shadows join—yours rising up from groundwater—

mine flung downward in dew.

≈

At sixteen. I want to beg you: Don't leave your viola on the pile of dirty clothes at your
　　　　　bedside where you will step through its delicate, tigerwood maple body—think
of music here as a splintered

gray dock where Grieg, Bach & Rachmaninoff share the same tenuous plank & every
　　　　　other board that keeps hold over Ox Bow Lake is named George Jones. Old
Possum has a fan club such

that if he's too drunk to stand up for his concert one man tapes his ribs straight & the
　　　　　other holds his microphone. But there is no repair shop for your instrument
in Newellton—when your plank

breaks you may well as *hang a wreath upon the door* for your awkward little concertos.
　　　　　Hang a wreath upon the door for your ignorance, while you're at it. If I
can start with getting you

to wash & fold your clothes I can save six men. Button back their jeans, starch & tuck
　　　　　their shirts, set them back to playing darts in that odd doll house, cut their
liquor with water, keep

you on the porch, make you practice harder. Wild bird, wild would-be daughter—I think
　　　　　if I can get you to put your viola in its crushed velvet case, proper, instead of being
so careless—I can save you.

　　　　　　　　That if I cannot go back & save you—
　　　　　　　　　　　　　　Music can.

II

Salt Hill

I was born in a Tennessee sanatorium hours after my mother's father died & I know
how the womb becomes a salt-sea grave.

I was born in the last seconds of small crops & small change rained down on the
collection plate's felt palate & I know

the soul's barn debt to past generations, too.

Outside, ditchfuls of chicory flashed in the after-rain sun as melancholia's purple
scent rose & its steepled fog distilled in Tennessee hills.

& I know I'm not supposed to be here on account of all those crazy aunts & I know
great grandma was five

when her Cherokee mother died & her daddy dumped her on the red clay curb
of an Arkansas reservation then drove away in a wagon—

how she just strode the fields of milkweed back to Tennessee & married her cousin.

When I was five I drowned a fly in a piepan of water then spooned it out & heaped
a hill of salt on its still body until I could hear a buzz again (as if within a belly)

& I know the rush of the resurrected.

I was born in the last decade of small town girls wearing white gloves to funerals.

As an infant my boy quit suckling long enough to wave to my mother's ghost—
who used to drift in the doorway of the hours.

& at three he told me at my age he had red hair & broke his neck falling off
a runaway horse—I know

the rocking chair's set too close to the edge of the porch.

Pretty Polly

Who made the banjo sad & wrong?
Who made the luckless girl & hell bound boy?
Who made the ballad? The one, I mean,
where lovers gallop down mountain brush as though in love—
where hooves break ground to blood earth scent.
Who gave the boy swift words to woo the girl from home
& the girl too pretty to leave alone? He locks one arm
beneath her breasts as they ride on—maybe her apron comes
undone & falls to a ditch of black-eyed susans. Maybe
she dreams the clouds are so much flour spilt on heaven's table.

I've run the dark county of the heart this music comes from—but
I don't know where to hammer-on or to drop a thumb to the
haunted string that sets the story straight: All night Willie's dug
on Polly's grave with a silver spade & every creek they cross
makes one last splash. Though flocks of swallows loom—the one
hung in cedar now will score the girl's last thrill. Tell
me, why do I love this sawmill-tuned melancholy song
& thud of knuckles darkening the banjo face?
Tell me how to erase the ancient, violent beauty
in the devil of not loving what we love.

Deepfreeze at the House of Boo—Who Told Me to Meet Her at 6 O'Clock so She Could Beat Me Up for Trying to Steal Her Boyfriend

—apologies to Galway

I stood at the end
of a gravel driveway between
flatlands & acres of trailers slapped-up
as temporary housing for migrants
who dreamed they'd stomp enough cotton
to get rich & build two-storied palaces
with satellite TV & in ground pools—
stood at the end, maybe,
to prove with a punch,
I could skin a coon
without crying, or be a good
hunter of men & saw for the first time
a deepfreeze on the lawn—
rain rusted, orange streaked

deepfreeze like the one Voncille Platt stored her outlaw gator meat in—
    I loved the tan-hide scent in her shed, I'd sometimes hear dactyls of rats
    gnawing through boxes of baby clothes—she's gone,
where Doris Barnes snuck in & cursed daddy to hell for beer-battering
    church-supper fish, then gifted us with bags of corn already locked
    in her own airtight box so long they tasted less food than gifts of
    freezer burn—she's gone,
where Candy Burnside went after school & learned to aim a gun because
    back then girls with degrees seemed useless as hounds that couldn't trace
    a scent—she's gone,
frozen in a landscape where deepfreezes don't outlive their use as porch

art or too-good hide-n-seek places for some kid who seals herself up
then shouts for hours before suffocating under a stuck lid—
    they're gone—
the girls & wives of Newellton who whistled through turkey calls, who
    cooked, canned & saved remains decades past expiration dates—

for the first time, so displaced—
the deepfreeze—like a couch on Jupiter or
like Mr. Otto's toolbelt slung on Mama Ray's porch
& I wondered if Boo would break my bones to fit
that ancient dented appliance
or would she let me off with a split lip—
her door opened

when I shouted: *Come on out and get some of this*—

if I had shut my mouth, then, instead
of letting that 90 lb version of Tammy Wynette
bruise *Stand by Your Man* into my face,
or dirty my shirt against
rocks stacked like deer hearts for flood
season when you'd eat the unimaginable not to starve—
but—
back then I thought I wanted Butch Merritt
who kissed like a beaver with four sets of teeth
& whose family owned the one sawmill to freedom
from there to New Orleans—so by the time Boo's daddy's
truck pulled in, I'd been clocked so dizzy I couldn't hear
the crickets' evening blaze.

Yes—a deepfreeze
with mildewed seams of summer
rising up from brutal weeds of that place—
a thing they'd not need in big cities where
I thought all there was to eat was brie
& folks passing by in Mercedes-Benz's would sneer
to see the same brokenhearted beast—its jaws unhinged
& emptied of all the marriageable dreams in Eden.

Might Mean Something

You cut the oildrenched pelican
 from the front of the *Times*
  & keep it in a box of things
   to save because it might. Like
    the Mayans—how funny they
     thought the conquistadors—
      charging in with soup-pots-
       for-hats—then the end came.
        Still it might not be an omen—
         for years you took in the plastic
          rings caught round the throats
         of seabirds till they became
        common as coral necklaces.
       & the rattlesnake granddad
      lifted into the canvas bag with
     tongs that summer escaped—
    but no one you know got
   swallowed whole. Ditto the pet
  boas let loose in the Everglades.
 Turns out you never needed
  the stash of embroidery hoops,
   the velvet cloth for the crazy
    quilt, material your mother
     could not bear to—you gave
      away. How do you choose?
       Whatever uncle Mayfield could
        not fit in the yellow jalopy out
         the front of his house where
        he slept with his foot on the
       brake & his bag of whiskey
      beside the gearshift, he
     threw away.

Pretty As You Please

Say you are smitten with Jamal, but turn him down
when he asks you to supper, because Hestersue says you've pegged the
wrong man, turns out he's the bastard of incest—his mom with his uncle—
& he's light in the loafers, besides. She's not sure, but hears he's got mono
& VD—a penis the size of a thumbtack, all hat & no cattle & he don't
believe in Lord Jesus. She's seen him drink milk out the carton—he says
the C word, cheats his own grandma at blackjack, once tied a cat by the tail
to a laundry line, eats pigfeet & smells like a deadman nailed to a skunk.

Then when you're night fishing the Mississippi & catching a bucket of nothing,
lonely as a single barge weeping its rust in the water—you see them—on a
bridge above you, hair slick as frogskin & glittering from skinny dipping—
as in bucknaked & necking—& suddenly the moon is an empty jar of mayo.

Mules

When they told us *Don't speak until spoken to*, we grew
ears the size of corn.

When they forced us to eat everything we swallowed
their hurt whole.

When they hit us for drawing on the wall we painted
doors that opened behind curtains.

For generations they lived like this. Wanting badly to
save us—not knowing how.

& all the while we found love in unlikely places: In
the ravaged church of our bodies & our faces,

refracted in their long faces.

Ether

I go back to my grandparents' house & see choked-up greens grandpa said eat
          or not leave the table, till I did. Grandpa's name: Ether: A flammable mix
of ethyl alcohol & sulfuric acid—or a drinker with a hard name to swallow.

I go back further & in Ether's shop I handle the razor strop he beat dad with
          while calling him a rat—single animal who'd eat a hubcap to live. & there
he is, my father—a small child cleaning engines by pouring gasoline over them.

Not what I want. I want to see the time grandpa jumps the stairs with a full wash
          tub & drenches the second story fire to save dad—an infant in his mother's
arms on the verge of burning.

                    Ether as compound has a sweetish scent.

I want to see where the horizon divides dark fields from lit sky in one clean line. But,
          barefooted, I find a half-swallowed frog some hawk dropped—viscous guts
along my arch. This happens, when I walk my father's fields—

I find the light: His busted watermelon rind & eaten-out heart—spat seeds of fruit,
          as a boy, he stole. A sweet beginning that ends in dark consequence: Lye soap
scalding his tongue. What is the horizon but

a strop laid so straight it obscures the curvature of the earth?

When dad was six, Ether said he wished the neighborhood stray dead & to please him,
          dad caught the dog & beat it with a hammer. There was not enough strength
in his childish grip to kill it, so it limped after him all these years—whining for

a final place to lie down.

I think grandpa didn't mean his wish, but evidence stacks against him. He kept a
          squirrel caged on the porch till it bit him, then he broke its back. What did my
child-dad see? & how like ether grandpa's wish must have been—you can cause

an explosion on the breath of its fumes. I go back to how grandma fell for him:
          He pulled her braids in the sandbox. Her parents tried later to douse those
flames. So the night train to North Carolina & her time hid away from him. But

each crossed tie ignited a spark. He climbs her braids.

She pulls him from a liquor barrel—not a hair of sense on her own head. I blame it on
          ether—love's anesthesia—how it leaves you mid dream, oblivious to pain.
Sometimes she'd pack up & leave Ether for some dark

thing he did—then go back for alchemical light so strong & imperfect you cannot
          understand it any better than you get the big bang—cosmos rising from
a single heat source. Primeval fern grown from ash. I go back

& cradle my child-father—who with the ardor of Jesus wanted to please his father—
          & the dog he did not yet know he loved. The bloodied fur becoming my hair
no one ever so gentle as my father brushed. Dad got named for the Morris

E. Henson Music Co. When I hear it, I see gold letters on a shop front window—
          a jamboree of bright pianos plays behind the glass—for the worst crime dad
committed against me was to offer an unripe persimmon: On my palate it

bittered with ether's residue—tincture similar to aspirin. Dad made our meals, housed
            refugees, ironed our jeans. When rabbits ate our strawberries down to roots he
said there should be enough to share with all & planted more. Ether also means

the all-pervasive, infinitely elastic, massless stuff

formerly supposed the medium begetting electromagnetic waves. I go back & grandpa
            gives me my first coke. I'm small enough not to know what's under that stuck
lid & laugh when shook carbon explodes—an oxygen tide bursts stars down my arms.

How exponentially love expands in even its smallest doses.

I go back to how dad might not live if for one less semen tithe between Ether &
            whatever meanness my grandmother withstood. Sometimes dad threatened
sudden death in the kitchen by holding his breath till grandma poured cold

water on him to *make* him live. That washtub of water in the burning house should have
            been too heavy for Ether to lift—if not for the supernatural. My father stands hip
deep in the lake of my dream one night—he holds the body

of a dog in one hand & in the other, its head. I ask him to sew it back. He pulls out a needle
            & thread. Begins. You have to eat a peck of dirt before you die, my parents said. I
thought I knew what the cliché meant: So many greens you face

down to leave the table for play. No, that's not it. There are harder things to swallow: Soap,
            cinders, knives. Here's a space to mourn love unrisen to earthly forms—scars
hardening into knots & knots-gone-petrified rock.

Grandpa dies. I remember his intoxicating laugh & grit. His hair, clear as ether, so light
        a liquid it ascends to water's surface & spreads. This is why you cannot put
an ether fire out with water—better to take a damp rag & press the man's face

that's mean enough to sober up & feed five kids when food was scarce. Better bury
        the flames in sand. The regions of space beyond earth's atmosphere comprise the
heavens—the ether. Better do as our mothers & fathers did: Thread a tough needle

& stitch the broken seam between the ether & this dark earth.

Tying the Knot

There ought to be a ceremony where the groom, stripped of his rented
    tux, zooms down the aisle on his motorcycle waving his holy, fetid socks.

His best man ought to be a too-often beaten dog, two spotted tails
    tucked between his legs, sour, bedraggled, late champion of tennis balls.

His song ought be rampageous as Mahler—brooding undertones of
    Wagner—the kind to turn from sun-blistered lake, to a dish of pallid water.

The sole bird of his faith's estate should be graffitied as a clown &
    like so many sunken vows, it should arrive dead on the plate of his tongue.

The bride ought to come discordant & contradictorily timed as Ives,
    wearing her black habit of granola soap & holding a bouquet of machetes.

Her maid of honor should be a once too-often tortured & high-strung
    monkey, tail stuck out between dress buttons, tacky, juggler of rancid bananas.

The rug unfurled beneath the bride's feet should be old as Methuselah—
    the kind to turn a summer stroll to a groveling crawl through wormwood.

The sole ride of her heart's carnival should be creepy as it is unknowable.
    As so many thrilling vows, it should rattle loose the church windowpanes.

O, the two should exchange brass manacles under a runaway train of tears.
    & the ushers should hand the guests bags of fleas to fling at the pair

as they disappear down the highway in a hot-pink, speedy-thrift hearse—
      so from then on, the marriage of those young & wild ones could scarcely get

worse. & their dull dinners across from each other wouldn't seem less
      miraculous than they are: Feasts of sweet, crusty bread, & strawberries soaked

in dandelion wine. & they would trade halcyon looks—common as rocks
      found in a field, comfortable as mud-loving sows & lasting everlastingly long.

III

Nocturne: So Mixed Up She Don't Know Day from Dark

For if we could hear
her while we slept, with her feathers, the owl swept dead leaves from the branch outside
our window & the spider collected, in her web, stray particles, or the mess of evening
dew. & our mother gathered up remnant undershirts, filled buckets with suds, scrubbed
baseboards, vacuumed floors, where all day we let the petals of our comings & goings
fall: Slips, nail polish, dolls. Or she baked while moths kneaded in the small yellow bowl
of porchlight—a fine layer of flour on their wings they couldn't shake off. A yeast scent
rose up through the floorboards & permeated our sheets, so our dreams came in neat
loaves we saw—but could not eat the intangible thing we wanted: Her earlobes, tendrils
of hair. & if the kitchen was a forest we walked into mornings, then from somewhere
under the linoleum a sinkhole must have swallowed our mother, her tracks still fresh by
the pantry—or else she folded her wings & slept, daylong, in a crack in the wall by the door.

I'll Wear the Hound out of That

As when the beagle flopped on the doorstep
        half dead from chasing the coon last night,
                what ring-tailed jailbreak, puddle romp
                        & fur-lined belly stuckled with cockleburs.

As when the snuffed-out sniffer never knew
        such confederate jasmine—vanilla scent full
                as a fatted tick—& perfumed chase exceeds
                        impossible capture: So river, so pine scent

leads on to loam & what rots beneath leaflitter—
        lacework of feather, fossil & bone—mingles with
                wild suckle. O yonder, nostalgia—once, a full
                        ditch bowl of babe rabbits & once, too eager,

a shrew bite to the nose. As when loving a thing
        you can't get too close to—so pant, so jowlful
                of appetite's salty spit, so runaway milk &
                        sorghum. As when Robby enlisted & Emmy

wore his dirty shirt as a daily commandment.
        Or this morning when you wanted to scold
                the delinquent animal of desire for leaving—
                        but brought her warm water instead, said

                        there now & soaked her threadbare paws.

Whiskey Pastoral

There were a thousand names for whiskey & only one for joyride
        when the sparkplug stars were supercharged. Only one word
for the cable wherefrom swung the shorn moon.

How should we describe the levee scent that was both oil & wool?

After we rolled the Jeep into a ditch & climbed out the window
        facing Venus & drew our hands clean down the bent frame's
hill to the valley so deep there should have

been a lake—& after we called for sheep in the dislodged bumper
        & looked down a twisted rubber lane to the undone hood—
we looked for the wolf in a crushed headlight.

Where the stone wall sank low enough that a wolf might climb over
        it, the wheel met the ditch. Where there were wolf-prints, a panel
of steel came apart from the inner workings

of the meadow. From below the dash the radio still bleated: *I'm crying
        icicles instead of tears* & the engine hauled a last bucket of bolts
& washer fluid. The meadow had much going

on we did not understand: The gizmo that opens a window to Lethe,
        the clicker that locks a door perfectly shut, why milkweed pods
explode in late October. Through the back

window our rifles still held in the crook of a rack. What could we tell
            our fathers? We'd have to walk to work. Could it be fixed:
The body soldered & painted to match

previous paint again? Happy accident. Were we herded into the last bunker-
            less pasture for just this: Cobwebs strung blue lyres between long
grasses, while a backseat cooler leaked:

White lightning
firewater
rotgut
grog
redeye
mule kick
block & tackle
sheep dip—

old tomahawk.

Don't Let Your Mouth Write a Check Your Butt Can't Cash

We should all be
so sure the check's in the mail & the cash in the bank & the bank in the black—

forgive me the promises I took back:

For I could not keep you, lover, entertained—I would give you the circus but when we
walked past, carnies pulled up their stakes & down the tent came—to stubs in the dirt,
crushed paper cups, one blue sequin stuck

to the heel of your boot.

& If not the circus I would give you music—a flamenco ukulele jamboree—sounded good
from the highway but entering late, we just caught the encore: *Heart & Soul* played on one
instrument & one string—

(a shoestring).

& if not a concert, I'd give you knowledge—of the physical attributes that make raptors
such excellent hunters. From the eyesight of eagles to the silent flight of owls. But that,
too, went fowl—at the aviary, falcons died mid flight—

so all the way back to the hotel we swerved to miss the bodies of falling birds.

Then the hotel burned.

& the bellhop fed a rope of sheets out our third story window to lower the cleaning girl down. & the ring I said I'd give you melted beside a plastic fundeck of kama sutra cards. Watching them from the street

you noticed the last knotted rung of rope that saved the girl was your silk blindfold & the bellhop might have flown out on a black plume of smoke—

                             had not flames caught

              tail feathers of my boa clenched
                          in his teeth.

Calvary Letter

That shell of our house in Calvary, Georgia no longer reminds me of the porch—
old couch & crush of blackberries,

empty-paned windows, cracked board of Lady Day's voice thrown into the musk-
dirt yard where we danced—

anymore than it reminds me of the kitchen rats & wire baskets of food hung from
the ceiling, or the jerry-rigged,

outdoor shower where we stood in mud to get clean—

or Solo, blind dog—the two patches of fur that rose like twin islands of grass from
his mange-bruised ocean of skin.

I want to say the reason one wayfaring bird flew all that way to sing on the rafter
over our attic bed is because

the roof was half missing,
an oak snake ghosted the mantle of the room below

& there was no other place so in need of restoration as the one where we lay
in a tangle of bliss:

Our faith—blind dog—our hope—hung basket—our vows—blank panes—ourselves—
cracked boards.

Can I say that house was a romantic, if irredeemable, mess?
That repairs overwhelmed us?
We cheated work to be done in places?

That we bought new faucets & you moved the stairway & tore down clapboard walls
to reclaim the floor no longer reminds me

of the vows we promised to fix from the foundation up—

you hinging my elbow back into place—
          me planing your spine to get it straight.

I want to say the reason sparrows smashed into the new sheets of glass is because
unstreaked windows are dangerous to birds

& tin roofs where the flashing's all plumb & gutters flush with the eves give
a false ring to rain.

What it does remind me of—that Calvary house—

is how many gallons of water could soak your wings—how many pounds of nails I
could hold in my beak & still not break.

Crazing

Every year I fire a vessel in a pit & call carbon rivers between finished glaze—crazing.
I call white plains between ash rivers—glaze—though you (dear one) may call
them whites of a witch's eye,

glacial plates, a desert of bones. I used to believe crazing was a shift in wind—seven
blackbirds on horseback—west-bound, galloping. A comet shattering a glass
palace of stars.

That was before you sent my letters back, each one, still sealed in its little coffin. Before
your children sat on a splintering bench & wept outside the asylum. Inside, I
stared into the rivers of your face

& saw the face Narcissus loved more than his own—the watery one that had no words.
I knew then that the horse, the comet were wrong—crazing does not move at
all, but waits for rain—

a single salvatory thing. I pull the vessel of each year out with tongs—the dents they
make in clay, deranged. Once clay goes into the fire it can't be reshaped or so they
say, but I don't

exchange their currency for pots—I give the vessels, the years, away. Wicked twin—I
give you away & you blaze over Dante's innermost ring of fraud—a field you
walked backward

through pig shit to get to—one littered with flags & graves for the masses (where lies
between us do the work of maggots). I hate the way you hitch me to your hell-bent
flames & we burn

down the houses of our children. Hair of soot. Soot on our tongues—every blackbird in
  our voice burnt still & dumb.

  ȣ

When I give the vessels away I say,

Now here's a piece you'll want to fill with flowers but can't because its walls are too porous to hold water.
   Where are you now? I've taken to reducing the pots in sawdust—dust of trees those
earthen bodies all

come down in a damp implosion of woodscent (infant cry of fall). Sometimes I wish the
   crazing on these vessels would not turn out—so beautiful—& every artist, then,
would choose

a plainer glaze—shapes that weren't so strange but felt good in the hands. Sometimes I
   wish the pots would break & I'd have nothing more to do with them: No more
rivers of ash & inverse plains.

You swing back to me in a dream overcast with ethereal light your hair so long it drags the
   dirt—your face an open envelope—your silent movie laughter thrilling down uncut
chords of sleep.

Sometimes we spiral back into the days raku meant: *Pleasure*. A wild wind knocks you into
   your pooled reflection & between your voice & vessel the gods poured it in—there's
no heat of separation.

Snow Angel

Tell me about ice & I will tell you about the bottle shard held to the boy's throat
        in my kitchen. He seemed to melt into the floor & the shard made
a scar on the tile where it missed its mark.

Tell me about snow—we'd looked for coke earlier that night but drowsed so drunk
        that instead of cruising Alabama Street for dealers we drove by the governor's
mansion. We hardly knew the difference

& would've stopped on that corner same as anyone's—had the boy not caused
        a skirmish with the driver & instead we short-cutted home. Mostly we swerved
the wrong side of the road—the same

side we drove down all year—though no one noticed on account of our being ghosts.

In the driveway—we did not want to get out of the car. Like when it's subzero
        & you have to move from your place by the fire & cross the frozen tundra.
The driver was unseasonably quiet. I hoped

the boy would shut his mouth. This was no arctic—we loved each other. In the yard,
        dogs barked & the house made the shape of a skull with no light behind
the eyes. Dope lay like Loa on the dash.

Tell me about sand & I will tell you how glass is made from flint, spar, iron, sea salt,
        pearlash, arsenic & wood ash. It was summertime in Louisiana. Before
the coke run we'd watched the century's

best meteor shower—the three of us wrapped in one sleeping bag by the gulf. Who
       knows how one thing becomes another? I can only recount the elemental
parts. Like when you lie with a lover,

shoulders touching & can't tell where the skin of one arm ends & the other begins.
       Inside on the divan the driver played guitar. I wanted to sleep. The boy toyed
with the ice in his jack & coke then broke

the silence with a stray remark. It had been a hard year, like I said, we were ghosts—
       we only saw each other. All summer drought so bad you couldn't toss
a cigarette butt out the window without
                    burning down a forest.

Tell me about stags meeting in the wilderness & I will show you how to lock antlers
       gracefully—no blood on the grass—one wins, the other loses, that's that.
No one died, we were already dead

from divorce, drugs, canceled checks & childhoods we could not get back. Of my
       kitchen I can tell you it's the place we most liked to gather—that the bottle
was blue as midnight's ocean—an ocean on

a table, then in the driver's hand—the boy on the floor & how resolution is the weather of
       fiction. Tell me of snow & I will tell you how soundlessly the body falls in slow
motion—how hard it is to cut

       a clean angel without leaving footprints when you try to stand up again.

The whole secret lies in the fact that it is quite impossible to tie a man while in a standing position, with such a length of rope, so that he cannot squirm out of it with comparative ease, if the tying begins at one end of the rope and finishes at the other.

—HARRY HOUDINI

Ingénue

Let there always be nights like this we prayed: The Word to lay on the palate long
enough that we may kiss—

because the glass cutter angled his window just so—moonlight shone through
a lamb's belly.

Because the house of our Lord had stiff wood pews hand hewn by slaves who put
the Holiness in that church

& Marvin Gaye's ecstatic radio-choiring of *Sexual Healing* was meant to commingle
with Handel's trumpet afterglow.

Because we sat cross-legged in a circle instead of warring over grief & oil or shoes
& everything else that made the blues, the blues.

                                       & last Sunday we forgot to give praise

to the starry navel sunk in the olive grove of girlishness, cinnamon lip gloss, new
boy's zebra thong strung above his Donatello hips.

Christ's blood smacked of strawberry wine when we were young & we knew grace
could spin & land on anyone.

Because even paired swallows make a nest of sticks in the highest arch beams &
crickets surely mate on the altar of dawn.

Leave It Lay Where Jesus Flung It

What a colossal wrong fall she took—that mastodon caught
several stories down in underwater muck thought:

Fuck. & wanted banjo—not this: Fretted plunge towards fossil—
sun's gold tone-ring diminishing. All summer archeologists

in wetsuits scope out ribs in the spring & miss the postmortem
marvel: Silver fingerpicks dart bone sockets, grow gills

in her sawgrass wrapped cranium. That's how bad she wanted
banjo—while sinking, archaeopteryx varmints circling

the surface. Small moon on which she strummed what would
evolve without her: Sparrow, savior, galax licks—air

bubbles blowing out her trunk. No not her trumpet—*What
a Wonderful World's*—bright brass belongs to Satchmo &

she'd die anonymous as pearl inlay or those heroines drowned
in murder ballads. For all eternity's a chorus of rogue

villains slipping roofies in your swamp when you're a mastodon
clawhammering a busted clavicle past the watery brink

of boomalacka while Cro-Magnons carve spears from the bank
& a butterfly sails past the alligator's teeth. All the world's

a neck drawn out the spring's belly where docked glass-bottom
boats rock & research teams mark the dig site with yellow

tape—a crime scene to beached yokels, sweating August for the
long dismembering. Soldout little snackshop & the diving

platform's closed. *Leave her bones* I want to say to the craneman
angling for a coccyx. What mastodon worth her salt would

want this climate controlled museum where she's headed, Muzak
streaming out the artificial cave? But the hook falls in with

a twang. Think you know what's possible? Each misstep unearths
a miracle: Where the mastodon's still double thumbing away

her last mistake—algid currents whorl a bridge from her left tusk.

Stars, As the Bride Who Could Not Tie the Knot Sees Them

☙

She lurks in the bayou—where emerald algae
slicks tree roots shaped
from a carnal rising of

        all things underneath—

                Still, still. There are places so vegetative—
                the brain thickens against all
                thoughts of self

& turns its ear to the other—

          fertile motion of crabs, peering behind tall
          grasses—open jaws of the alligator
          approaching turtle eggs.

                All creation is for nothing—

unless it is for the one burning star who leaves
her intimates of light strewn in every
dark room of the gods.

～

From shore the bride who might have been sees
        the groom who did not choose her, paddle away

in a johnboat. She wishes him well, she uses all
        her wishes—wishing he would have everything

he wants & while she's wishing, twin breasts the
        size of Everest rise from the water's edge, so

the groom drifts through a canal of cleavage.
        Mullet swimming by him wax gold as they fling

themselves over the side of his boat, which begins
        to sink from the weight of all the groom's wishes

unexpectedly coming true. & now the groom grows
        dark as the anhinga of night who dries his wings

along the horizon. & now a new moon. From here,
        the bride who might have been sees the silhouette-

groom in water up to his knees, grope for all the
        golden loot he can hold & release it on the deck

of Charon's ferry. Charon—lone satellite of the
        coldest planet—are you the last wish of the leaving

groom, or are you the wagon of stars the bride who
        might have been hitched her own spent wishes to?

For every star the bride who would have been sees—millions more lay mute under her deep
        train of grief.
                        Love, she thinks, is a star whose sole calling is to bear the hurt of
erasure when daylight pulls a veil between it
                                & the bride it aches to glimmer towards.

 She knows the fallacy in this—the stars, love—indifferent to her face. That is why
        she shreds her veil
                                & flings the hazy streamers into trees—so what one gazes on
in the swamp's cypress limbs
                        are veil remnants woven into an osprey nest.

Moss—we say, when we see that silvery trail of lace shifting in wind over water.
Stone—we say, when we see the bride's abandoned altar.

& every time we call a thing by its name it disappears—if only we could see her, the
        bride would pelt
                        us with her moccasins each time we leave her at the church of her
brief existence. The moss, the stone have no name.
                                The would-be bride weeps: Look at *me*.

আ

How I love the anointed hour when sulking ends—

I love the absence of plush coffins

& how the fish caught under a rock becomes a food most infinite, divided between other
fish & diving pelicans.

The bride who might have been undoes the bows of her unopened gifts

& under each lid she finds an ivory bone carved into an iron she cannot use for an iron—
a lamp she cannot use for a lamp—

or some other artifact she cannot use for a life she will not live.

She carves the iron
into small
arrows—

   the lamp—
      into a new form
        that amuses nothing more
       than those swerving suns:
      Her hands.

≈

Welcome to the dark X-rated scene—the scene on the cutting room floor—

the wedding guests of the bride who would have been are chained
to the mouth of an underwater spring—no one knows who bound

them there—but they are dying. The grandmother in the amethyst gown

dies for the child who might've washed her car & the groom's father
dies for the last name he etched on the banks of Ellis Island.

The bridesmaids' hairpins fly out, their curls unfurl like eels lunging

towards the mates they will not meet in the partyless current. Mean-
while the bride's made off like an evangelist. If she could speak she'd

tell them to do as she & the falling stars

                                        have done for eons & get over it.

&

In the center of a stand
of virgin pines,
one night,
I saw her
cling to a tree,
so loftily thin—
it was the very hour's hand
swept across the clock of the moon. Since then—

I have known where falling stars
fall, when they fall
they land—
small heavens,
each one—
on the tongue
of the bride who might have been.

She did as the first Chinese brother had done—
held a vast yellow sea—

of all the fallen stars
in her mouth
so the sky grew perceptibly darker all at once—

when I looked to the night again, all the
chaste maids
of Pleiades had flown—

& in their place—
a bodice of stars undone—I looked to the tree, the bride was gone.

Letter to the Dark

I write you on a host of unseen things: The fine impression of bones dissolved in the face of a stone—

on tendrils of incense allemanding through the first ambrosial jasmine, verdant & white-starflower spring.

    The water in play beneath a frozen river.

I write you on the hair of space parting to make way for the barge of my heart to move on past an outworn parchment of:

Small town fairs of sheep.
Hardware stores, their sawdust scent & basketfuls of penny nails.
Patina gilding courthouses' copper domes & bells tied to adjacent gallows.

Sometimes trees reaching to touch over houses empty themselves of atoms so I may write you on the crawl-space of insects.

Whole nights pour out their prisms of thought so I may write you on all of night—

& even now I write you on the crystalline ladder of light the indigo swallowtail climbs from the roots of dawn into this full-blown morning.

A Coon's Age

It can't be told by height, lbs.,
           tooth count or tail rings—

but how long ago some
           settler named Tallahassee for

her old fields. Or how long the
           bar we walked to stood open-

doored so mosquitoes woozed
           in—but more time than it took

the blue lights affixed to pool
           tables to zap them. If you can

imagine how many oyster shucks
           it took to pave under the trucks

of the bayside fish markets or
           how many gallons of water pour

forth from the caves under
           Wakulla Springs. Longer than

the divorcees' chain of rings linked
           round the stag's horns in Kent's

bar & more than limbs in the
           streets after hurricanes—or how

deep the water to wade through,
         on Gains St. How long it will take

the hired goats in the mall parking
         lot to digest the strand of kudzu

twined round every last live oak.
         & said with a pang of missing:

Especially apt after two New York
         winters spent longing for drawls,

boiled peanuts, sweet cashiers, gold
         teeth & passion plays acted out

in front of churches. I keep your
         banjo pick tucked in my brastrap—

& last week the creek rose with all
         the ice melt, so I pulled last fall's

frozen coon's carcass from under
         the porch lest the thaw have him

stinking worse than skunks in heat—
         but he just grinned like a mule eating

briars, rared, then bit me.

The Last Resort

                    Underneath her front door, my neighbor's cries
must have billowed, evanescent as smoke, for hours. Naked,
she'd mounted the knob of her banister & got stuck. Dawn
  came before the firemen arrived to saw her down from her unlikely
stalk. Tonight the rain outside my bedroom window keeps me awake—
  then the query, what makes one wed the staircase? Leaf shadows
  move across a screen & I imagine the woman waltzing in the empty
  arms of space & wishing for a more physical presence to hold
  her—a hand, a rail to press the small of her back. In the years I
  lived alone, I dreaded the dark house so much I cruised the city
  parks or slept in the car not to go in. On the world's other edges
  it is not so different—we are coming to the last resort. Southward,
  someone's holed himself up in a state capitol & demanded SWAT
    bring him pizza, 666 Krispy Kreme donuts & ten cigarette cartons.
To the west, another man's tied his lawnchair to 45 weather balloons
  & floated 15,000 feet into LA airspace then shot himself down—
  saying: *A man cannot just sit around.* & in the Northeast? I think I hear
  a surge in the creek—rain hardens into hail on the roof & this is just
  July we're talking about—there are not enough blankets in all
    the world. After my divorce, I went to a party hopped-up on so much
    cough syrup that the barbecue flames resembled a flower & when
  I leaned to touch it, my hair caught fire. Running for water,
   I hit the glass door, & once inside, tumbled over a woman, whose
   arm I broke. That's how the year went: One emergency vehicle
    chasing the next until I smashed into the side of an ambulance &
    could not remember what name to give the police. A stranger
    pulled me out of the heap & sudden as a hailstorm in July we were

in love. Weeks passed before I learned he was only seventeen &
therefore what he did so well to me required a parent's permission
slip. I can hardly bear

                    to imagine my neighbor's position—naked
petal caught in the shame of her boredom or loneliness—a host
of men in Kevlar coats singing the chorus for what we don't
understand: *Sorry, Ma'am.* You have to laugh—when you come
to the last resort—it's the one place left where you can order up
what you most want & have it with mint, but you have to cross glacial
plains vaster than the scar on Mars to get there & when you do—
the desk clerk demands your last dime of wit to stay for more
than a day. Both the man in the capitol room & the one who aimed
his lawnchair towards Jupiter eventually shot themselves. Storm
winds blow open the upstairs doors as if the travelers of my own
regrets break in to say the chimney's cracked & the fire leaks—they want
it fixed or else their money back & what's in the cash drawer to give
is my son's words to me this morning in the hammock when I asked
if I could read him a story? No, listen—he said, & you can hear it
                                (birches rustled, birds warbled).

Small Cosmos

I've seen a wheat field riven where an almighty finger of wind flicked a silo into
the green sky like it was an aluminum flea vaulted towards oblivion—

grain showered the ant & shrew alike & in the wake of disaster—even the gopher
turtle shook the dirt off her nose, to eat.

Should I love a ruined family of giants more than I love the unasked-for blessing
befallen to the smallest creatures?

(To see a thing riven is to wish I'd given you one brass button for luck.)

I've heard a river waltz through laced hands of the levee toward a grand new
partnering of earth & water—

then stood for weeks in the tenebrous waters of that breaking, wondering,

> would my own feet ever dry enough for dancing?

Men with shirts tied round their waists waded over highways with buckets &
plunged makeshift spears into flashing fish—were they poor men?

It makes no sense to speak of the poverty & riches of love. Love,

come as a cloud & I will stay in the country below you. If you are, by night,
a fire, I will follow your fragrance of ashes into the wilderness.

I will eat your cornbread, pomegranate & fig. I will put away my ghosts & move into whatever stone house you provide—

even if it means learning a new way of speaking. Out of hammered silver, I send two trumpets with which you may call me.

Book Benefactors

Alice James Books and Jane Springer would like to thank the following individuals who generously contributed towards the publication of *Murder Ballad*:

Anonymous

For more information about AJB's book benefactor program, contact us via phone or email, or visit us at www.alicejamesbooks.org to see a list of forthcoming titles.

Recent Titles from Alice James Books

ALICE JAMES BOOKS has been publishing poetry since 1973 and remains one of the few presses in the country that is run collectively. The cooperative selects manuscripts for publication primarily through regional and national annual competitions. Authors who win a Kinereth Gensler Award become active members of the cooperative board and participate in the editorial decisions of the press. The press, which historically has placed an emphasis on publishing women poets, was named for Alice James, sister of William and Henry, whose fine journal and gift for writing went unrecognized during her lifetime.

Designed by Dede Cummings
DCDESIGN

Printed by Thomson-Shore
on 30% postconsumer recycled paper
processed chlorine-free